# Cat Lady Librarian's Cats

## Brenda S. Parris

Cat Lady Librarian's Cats
Cat Mama Librarian's Cats, Book 1





ISBN: 9798993997650 (hardcover)
ISBN:  9798993997636  (paperback)
ISBN: 9798993997643 (Kindle eBook)
Back Home Books
Decatur, Alabama
backhomebooks.info
brendasparris.com


Illustrations done by the author
using ChatGPT/DALL-E and Canva

In honor of
Cocoa, Tiger, Misty, and Elsa
and in memory of
Midi, Patch,
Autumn, Spring, Summer,
and Angel

I am a librarian
and some say I'm
The Crazy Cat Lady.
I have four cats now.
I have had six at a time
several years ago.

Tiger
Elsa
Misty
Cocoa

I'd like to introduce you
to Cocoa, Tiger, Misty and Elsa,
and tell you how
they came to be with me.

Cocoa and Tiger

I adopted Cocoa and Tiger from
the local animal shelter
soon after my two boy kitties
Midi and Patch passed away.

Cocoa is solid black and big,
and he helps me keep
Tiger out of the closet.

Tiger is a gray tabby, long and slim,
and he is my physical therapist kitty.
He helps me do my post-knee replacement
exercises every morning.

Misty is solid black, with long hair,
and a long fluffy tail.
She is so small she can sleep on my back,
just like Angel, who was sick and
soon passed, had done.
She was a stray that kept visiting my patio.

Elsa is a solid white blue-eyed beauty.
She belonged to my friend, Deb,
who left her with me when
she moved back home to Iowa.
She is Queen of the Living Room.

In the next few books
I will let each of them
tell their stories.
Stay tuned!

# It's a true story ...

I really am a librarian, at a community college, and I really do have four cats. Their names really are Cocoa, Tiger, Misty, and Elsa. They each have their own very different personalities. And they each have their own stories. Stay tuned as they each tell you their stories in their own books coming soon!

Cocoa
and
Misty

# Tiger and Elsa

# Tiger and Elsa

# Cocoa and Misty

# Cocoa and Misty

Do you have cats?

If so, how many?

What do they look like?

What are their names?

Do you know anyone else who has cats?

If so, what do they look like?

What are their names?

Can you write about them?

Write down some ideas.

You might write a book someday.

# Books about Cats

Abdale, Denise.  *A Tale of Trust and Love: a Children's Book about Two Feral Cats' Journey from Abandoned to Adopted.*  (Adventures of Pickles and Rufus). Independently Published, 2025.  ISBN: 9781968701024

Allenby, Victoria.  Nat the Cat Can Sleep Like That.  Pajama Press, 2014. ISBN: 9781927485521

Apollonio, Marietta.  Jack the Library Cat.  Albert Whitman, 2021.  ISBN: *9780807537510*

Emmons, Lauren.  *No Cats in the Library.* Simon & Schuster/Paula Wiseman Books, 2024. ISBN:9781665933681

# More Books about Cats


Kiser, Teresa. *Dewey's Tale.* Public Library of Anniston-Calhoun County, 2024. ISBN: 9798332157486

Laminack, Lester L. *A Cat Like That.* Margaret Quinlan Books, 2025. ISBN: 9781682635230

Louch, Jan. *The True Tales of Baker and Taylor: the Library Cats Who Left their Pawprints on a Small Town ... and the World.* Thomas Dunne Books, 2016. ISBN: 9781250081070

Martin, Bill, Jr. *Kitty Cat Kitty Cat Are You Waking Up?* Two Lions, 2008. ISBN: 9780761454380

Myron, Vicki. *Dewey the Library Cat: a True Story.* Little, Brown Books for Young Readers, 2010. ISBN: 9780316068710

# Even More Books about Cats

Myron, Vicki. *Dewey: the Small-town Cat Who Touched the World.* Grand Central Publishing, 2008. ISBN: 9780446541190

Myron, Vicki. *Dewey: There's a Cat in the Library!* Little, Brown Books for Young Readers, 2009. ISBN: 9780316068741

Obuhanych, Karen. *This Little Kitty.* Knopf Books for Young Readers, 2023. ISBN: 9780593435144

O'Byrne, Nicola. *Bad Cat.* Candlewick Press, 2021. ISBN: 9781536217285

Sabol, Terri. *Oscar and Emmy Get Rescued.* (Oscar and Emmy series). Independently Published, 2016. ISBN: 9781946428004

Wenzel, Brendan. *They All Saw a Cat.* Chronicle Books, 2016. ISBN: 978-1452150130

9 7 9 8 9 9 3 9 9 7 6 3 6